A Pilgrim's Poetry

This is an IndieMosh book

brought to you by MoshPit Publishing
an imprint of Mosher's Business Support Pty Ltd

PO Box 4363
Penrith NSW 2750

indiemosh.com.au

 A catalogue record for this work is available from the National Library of Australia

https://www.nla.gov.au/collections

Title: A Pilgrim's Poetry

Author: Jeffs (SSF), Noel

ISBNs: 9781922912329 (paperback)
              9781922912336 (ebook – epub)
              9781922912343 (ebook – Kindle)

Subjects: POETRY / Subjects & Themes / Inspirational & Religious;
              BODY, MIND & SPIRIT / Mindfulness & Meditation

No individual in these poems is taken from real life. Any resemblance to any person or persons living or dead is accidental and unintentional. The author, their agents and publishers cannot be held responsible for any claim otherwise and take no responsibility for any such coincidence.

Cover concept by Noel Jeffs SSF.

Cover design and layout by Sarah Davies at https://lemondesignstudio.com.au/

Cover images used under licence from Adobe Stock.

A Pilgrim's Poetry

I celebrate this day

1990 — 1993

Noel Jeffs SSF

Also by Noel Jeffs SSF:

Maturing in the Religious Life

Walking in Stealth: After Pushkin

Contents

These three cycles of poems were written at Hilfield Friary in Dorset, England, at Rome and Assisi in Italy, and at St George's College Jerusalem, and in their environs.

The Epilogue was written prior and yet seems suitable to bear that title.

I am grateful for the listening ears of many friends.

If there is a constant theme throughout, it is the one which I find in the life of St. Francis of Assisi, that his life in search of God was a search for a father, which brings together the spheres of spirituality and sexuality.

The Hilfield Cycle

In this bridal way—in the
search for the Beloved; who
shall sort the seeds but 'the
bridegroom who cometh in
the night'? The transcendent
function comes to scatter all
the leaves.
Is desire sufficient to delight him?

Eros and Psyche shall match.
She with the path before her
must trust in all that the mother
of the deep has laid before her.
Each unsteady step brings its
wariness of shadows, and the
constant fear of falling.

These small flint stones were
sculpted in earth's cauldron of
fire, to be the beads of my wild
walk. (If every seed could talk?)

~ ~ ~

By cross and hand, my flight was
marked, in whose Christ-like
hand the torment was held by
webbed reins. By the fingers of
the contrite, and the starlit
apparition that shone through my
night; It was—to heed the call—
'rejected by men'; So I wept forlorn.

To slice the dolomite ,
to within and without,
making a darkness and
wonder how (in all) this
makes man.

~ ~ ~

I said I must go to the well. I journeyed
over hill and vale, along the bridal path,
descending the steps to meet the road and
watching the town come large, past the
giant of the phallic night: Him upright with
raised arm, to come to Augustine's well in
The Cerne of our Fathers.
Here I joined in oracle for healing and wish:
washed my face and soused the ardour.
O woman of the well,
All is known and in you foretold, that
love awakens the heart to swell.

As though in wandering, the wash; a washing
in moonlight's silver sheen and now to speak of
thou and I, And so clear is the homeward
journey carried by my tired feet; the three-fold
story of a child;
With father and son in Trinity.

~ ~ ~

And now I sat waiting for the
silver light and listening for its
tune:
'the bridegroom cometh in the morning' And
is this full moon?
Cursed be the story that fills my plate
and is no ladder to the moon——Alas to
him who hides the soft light that
shines from my pate.

Awake my soul, awake lute and harp.

For my God of whom is foretold at

the zenith; were all things that I hoped

for, would tell us a tale of these three

as embraced by the Bethlehem of old

at thy nadir,

beneath that starry night,

With its compass lobe and listening ear.

~ ~ ~

The Glory of the son shall be revealed.

In the Beloved is found both father and son:

Each as love-able; a crucible which makes renown.

'Sit thou at my right hand'.

Such endearment is fondness for evermore, whose

wellsprings bring

intimacy in the love of each other.

And in the oneness is twined a darkness
beyond our time.
In this language which is binary,
Jesus Christ is the timeless mirror
for every creature of God and Earth.

The Assisi Cycle

The Grail's Message to Amfortas.
"By his pity knowing, the pure fool,
Wait for him whom I have chosen."
[From Wagner's Parsifal]

~ ~ ~

The Holiday in Italy

A blue, earth-faltering sky
collapsed into darkness ringing
the dome of San Pietro.
Learn my Latin, and quickly too!
This is Roma, centre of
civilisation and mother of the
seas, in her whipped and chaotic
tide, with ever gushing streams.

I wandered lonely and wondering 'why?'
had said my prayer in the overwhelming
basilica before the small and strong, A
mother and her child.

Sometime parent, sometime child—and
together; fraught with my budget and
with its mine: an economy. Am I strong
enough to carry, the tide?

The endearing desire for others, comes
so strong—but here am I rolling before
the sun, doting on the pensiones, and
thinking of Il Duce and King Vittorio
Emmanuel:
the chequered flag of history and
wondering what it won. The
family: the sign, and all that civilise.

What is a good-enough mother?
What vale and mountain makes
an island strong?

To stroll in this archaic glory that was Rome,
of the Palatine Hill, forum, senate and
Colosseum; where the slain measure the
building blocks, And the ruins are their
recall. New life is springing green through
the creviced stones, where copious voices
once hallowed the round and its patricians
exalted their demeanour.

To wander in the alone
and note in each step
the conflict as it unfolds.
'Buona Sera Father' And he passed by! To
wonder in the hunger of the creativity that
gathers in this ground, "Am I Christian,

really?" and yet alive in the lather
that brows my mind and grinds me down.

Stigmata

As I ascended the hill,
to Assisi's citadel, my
heart murmured,
I have come thus far,
'This is it. One little crossroads!'
'Where stands my life now?' A
Celtic saint held my hand so faint,
and with a murmur crossed my
palm. So stands my life at this poor
gate, gasping in its withers and
craving as though beyond restraint.
Who dreamed the dream that
beckoned me to the Rocca, with its
call, the call to recreate. Well head,

and fountain head, this is the

erection of all; and nothing is

beyond its recall.

Here stands my masthead and my pall.

~ ~ ~

Hear as fool, that ignoring of the desire; that

orifice that yearned as from all my soul.

—I was afraid.

This was Joseph's walk in Egypt.

Surely now as both a parent and a child—'I'.

To murmur and to hold; together as

providing base and beckoning, from which I

might glimpse the eclipse,

of the landscape by the sun,

caught within its charm.

Here I stand ready to make

one step more and out, to

gather new raiment and
fragrance of angel's dust.

To have and to be held by the cool murmuring waters of
this sacred grove, where stand the encircling trees which
cast their deep shadows
over the chatter of the dead, wreathed by the smile of the
benign Francis; whose enchantment communes with
time — where all stands still.
So my pilgrimage is set in the passion of the
Father and the Son.

~ ~ ~

They said in the street to
one wandering friar,
'So young and so poor!' They did not
grasp the nettle with all its thorns, of
human suffering, whose pregnancy
contains this comedy of life's truth

where lust and power and money erase

love's poignancy and even lovers hide

love's clarion call. Hilarion!

The passion of the father and the

passion of the son.

One rose blooms where springs from the desert ran, and

earth yielded its tears. Leaving the city, the town and the

civitas, in his ears hearing the cry 'possessed' and to

search for warm and living stone, to transform and

capture in embracing arms all anger and all fear: and

from their embers fan a warmth so inflammatory to

flame, skip and girdle this whole round world; —

succoured in the Other and breadth of human love with the

grace of compassion and its understanding.

Below me flows the Rivo Torto, dredged

from the snow this little torrent of

ceaseless praise, becoming a mighty sinew

of endless days.

Il crescendo into the valley of despair and endless over-
eating, where anger has no real air.

I carved my track to the ravine of the Carceri;

the rock holes which have become the lair and ground of the

saints; (Their grottoes are there.)

And further into the glades of the forest beyond, whose

pines bathed by a fair sun, made shadows

with their silent whispering with room for

mating, and for each lover's care and

conversazione.

There was a needled walk to return for the gathering of

vespers at San Damiano amidst

the olive groves,

Where I was to be reminded as the child as

though as the one so ill prepared by a parent who was

there Him, Italian, roped and vowed,

whose daunting forbearance was to my mind covering his

ignorance—and so I stumbled in.

my humiliation and cursed where no words

could be heard and my entreaty was lost over differing

languages and with the stopped ear.

My tears washed the hillside until its slopes

lapped with salt in the vale's plein air.

~ ~ ~

The Portiuncula: A Little Portion. Where

has sprung from one ground, two shoots and

one rose passion of the father and pattern of

the son. A crown and royal diadem, marks

the space where all began, and I found

myself as the father's son.

PS 142 (Parsifal — Wagner) you see my son, time becomes

space here.

To Abbazia San Benedetto, a
weary walk of winding road
under the clout of sky and sun.
Whose gift, the rose garden
grew like a bubbling spring
with a world in view. The
message of those on the way,
in giving direction, could give
no ground to sow, to dispel
the dryness and the echoing
emptiness of one run down,
and fallowed long ago. So it
lies among its trees a memory
with other animals in its
nature reserve; where stones
are cultivated for future
generations to see.

No food to feed, nor seed to scatter to the wind.

The path, so lost by Tre Fontane and the bolted

gate at the Carceri, in its pause represents a discontinuous

tale. There bequeathed to posterity from its forest vaunt,

the trompe d'oeil of father/son has become another of

Calvary's fallen trees.

~ ~ ~

The father and the son is a story told often

and true in a search for identity. Yet every

child seeks its peers; of the story, siblings

and from those who come near, some as play

friends; where to play and run and with

minds at ease away from the privileged place;

the seat and the comfort of the feet of a

beloved master.

I could not make the walk today to the
cimetière——a level journey so it appeared for
what I sought, but I wasn't meant to be there. My resting
place shall be with the wolf at Gubbio; for him, a home and
to hear the diminishing cries of his despair.

The journey seems so vague and unclear
yet flurried desire brought to life an
agenda in objets d'art , and its suspire; a
bambino.

To smile back at me and me to learn the art. The praise of
moon and stars and endless dream and with the clear
guiding light of St. Clare; to guide the father and the son
and wash it in the moon's clear and shining stream. I
bought myself that bambino, so it could smile back at me. I
walked the journey to bus to Gubbio, so the wolf might lick
my ankles and warm its body around my knees.

I knew the father bound me tightly.

I wondered whether I had wandered too far!

Over the Appenines by a sinuous trail with its

cut and thrust, through frost and snow I went to the

haunt of the lone wolf, to find a hearth without trove.

Had I brought him to wrest and challenge again where

love makes green and my cry can be

heard once more. Dare I then venture to the cimitière to

wash his grave with my tear?

Shall I hold the events of life with a purview, to sunder its

treasure in an awakening, and cast my pearls before

Jerusalem and Calvary's due?

And dare I say to Gubbio, 'My heart was not with you,'

'And I dare not face you again,' In the bitterness where ice

thawed and blood ran again, and all that in a wan winter

sun where through crystal and icicle, was brewed a hope of

the world anew.

How can I thus journey, when it seems

the flight is too long and the connections are unsure?

for no one can see my anxiety—or hear it and pity so,

that there is understanding. Why do I live the night long

accosted by this anxiety—with no existence anymore, and

with a loss of temporality which makes my mind sore.

Travel, travel, the pilgrimage to beyond glass:

a wall against which the butterfly beats its wings. The

metamorphosis of life's healing spaces into a forward

resting place.

The Jerusalem Cycle

The gates which descend, in tiers, as steps
of conflicting humanity, in peace and with
quarrelsome voices, tunnelled through the
streets of this cavernous body. Here we
walk as a noisy throng, the bazaar; our
song. The streets abound in questions; as
yet unanswered and non-directive. These
are the streets which bound the man to his
destiny; and gave a mouse to the lion's paw.

~ ~ ~

The rigours of Mt. Sinai; its starlit,
light-shine, height of theophany,
holds a beacon where heart springs
enlighten a body and old moorings

cease; so shall freedom arise from the
ashes and from its girdings release:
and all this from the rock.

~ ~ ~

Faint hearted—quiet in the stillness of time;
not wanting to walk to Bethany, sitting from where I can
see the castellated towers of the city, and its pine trees: one
dusty crop. Cavernous is the emptiness, of my cisterns,
after the night's release.
The stuttering flags, pennants of that primeval battle, are
fluttering in a morning breeze.

~ ~ ~

Holy Mountain of Moses, the pad of rock upon
rock. A starlight's minaret; the spindle upon
which thread for the world was spun, to bower

the enchanting fire in blazing bush and
mirroring of the sun.
Carry my exalted heart, in its burnished bronze, and
arrow my shaft, for labour's
toil is love's braid; to strengthen the arm
and rivet the crag.

O star of Bethlehem,
mirrored on the ground,
sinkhole of its wanderings,
gathering a new birth and
creating the living God. O
star of the sea, whose
melodious calling is an
allure that continues to
weave, through note and
symphony, a melody of
me; through firstly the
mute arrival as the donkey

of all; Now humility tums
its wheel as the projected
are recalled.

~ ~ ~

I grapple with the stone of anointing, and

clutch my grief shroud, hearing the message of stupor;

overarched by my miserable cry; a lament of anger's

bitterness / I came to

Jerusalem so that I could die——a carnation's

brief glory, and I wonder why——so I toil in

loneliness, alone, and for the espy: the crisp gratification

of knowing that loveliness is my

soil and God is my die.

The pilgrim's steps are weary,
and record the rise and fall of the
heart in pitching tent; Hid by
these leafy glades, where the
unhurried quietness once
belonged to a pregnant maid.

Paradise lost, where emblematic of the desert
Elijah gathered crumbs as its crop.
Ravens hint at past shadows, where the
timeless land was a wandering heart. New
bread from heaven; the food giving flock
stations the call in the cavernous rock.
Here Samuel's plight in its insistence amidst Eli' s
slumbering night becomes the instigation to
redeem my lot.

Round and round we walked
Jericho's walls wishing its fall. City of old,
merchants and bazaars, rushing busy,
conflated by its pain and sorrow, maddened by
flies and despair, in the decadence of its self-destructing
bile. Rivers of sewage run down
to the sea, and here they fish.
Girded by its containing walls, this
is a pretty place of sandy shores on
the Mediterranean.

Where has the poetry gone? Too awful is
the truth; this is a concentration camp,
where lives dependent upon the whims
of others, dart in their chaos and
confusion lives knee deep in squalor.
Dare they forget the God, of life and
gratitude?

Old and young had then gathered
as kindred to anoint history as
one life's story and in the
embrace find the tears that
gladden and smart.

Now where bells ring and
new resonances sound, the
donkey makes its bray and
birds break the air with their
twittering cries. For me this
vale bursts forth with a desert
song of locusts and wild
honey, and the trumpeting
call of the mating ram.

The bridge through the
impassable, girding the
chasm and finding our
passage in the sweet
water pools of Jordan's
Rift: where repentance
brought its refreshment,
and the evergreen tree,
which budded crimson:
and flowered mightily,
in its fragility.

Paradise regained and once at the end of the
street is the slammer.
One fish crawled out of the sea to
try new land:
a net webbed with many pieces, fishes, loaves
and heavenly food. Jerusalem, Jerusalem, you
who stone the prophets, will your heels bruise
this head?

This Holy Mount where festal garments merry the throng,

helps the pilgrim to discover his song, within the mountain

air. Call thy tune now and capture the victor's ear.

~ ~ ~

St. Peters denial is thrice, and the

cockerel's crow like a dice remains a

lasting portrayal. That you are one, and together you are

born, as a part of me,

victim and bride of a world's mercilessness.

Out of the rock you were drawn, like a

fresh and flowing stream.

You were hewn from the rock.

The father and I are one.

The nebulous becomes significant,

When breeding and heeding the identification
which has made life forlorn, and even bilious
as filial. This now brings repentance as tears
of gladness make their song.
'Am I my father's son?' From curse of
crown of thorns; from Gethsemane's
laver trickles the stream of Bethlehem
to its Olivet. Thus fed by bitter herbs;
my discovering in the covenant is how
thanksgiving's excellence, is a cornerstone
for conversion's smile. For sacrifice is made
bone fide, when we have walked the extra mile.

~ ~ ~

I don't know whom I am?
A father and a son, who
met in yesterday:
in love's embrace, and even sacrificed
a life; for love is very death. This

union writ against the lore of the stars,

shook my core, and distinction made

us apart, and perspiration's dread

speaks of the bizarre. For all things

new confound old plots, and life-

giving dimensions seed new ground.

This is my winter's crop.

Epilogue

Child of God, flooded in beams; Rays of sunshine. God
shine. Moonshine and illuminated in truth forever. Wrap
this child in your warmth lying on water's
pondage, robust and alert helpless and silently inert:
afloat on the plane of lily leaf and pad.
Now held in mind; a world, over a
spout and fern of pain:
whose pity; a water rising whorl is enfolding the golden
dye over limbs and bower. To be another gumnut babe; this
birth of gilded limbs and lily flower. This child and orb
becomes its chrysalis and silken purse, of a torn woven
grail, lighting a day when gorging caterpillars develop
wings; whose unfolding in their sheen is to become the
prince of play.

Postscript

Some references in the poetry require elucidation:

1. The cross and hand (p. 2) though now only a stump of stone, is an ancient monument on the highroad above Hilfield Friary in Dorset in the United Kingdom. It features in Thomas Hardy's novel Tess of the D 'Urbervilles. Details and photos at https://historicengland.org.uk/listing/the-list/list-entry/1118653

2. En Kerem, (p. 25) beyond Jerusalem is popularly considered to be the site of the Visitation of Mary, the mother of Jesus to her cousin Elizabeth and the birthplace of John the Baptist.

3. St. George's Monastery, (p.26) in the Wadi Kelt between Jericho and Jerusalem is asserted to be the site where Elijah was fed by the ravens.

4. 'Jericho' is a metaphor of Gaza and the Gaza strip (p.26).

About the Author

Noel Jeffs SSF is an Anglican Friar originally from Gippsland, Australia. He is a sometimes student of Kate Lilley and others for a Master of Creative Writing at Sydney University. He is a disabled person living alone who enjoys conversations and silence and writing. Noel has a master's degree in Mental Health and has trained as a psychotherapist.

His two recent publications, 'Walking in Stealth: After Puskhin' and 'Maturing in the Religious Life', are available to be purchased through online bookshops, and his poetry compilation 'Under the Dome' is still available from Garden Lounge in Newtown, Sydney. He has been published in Burrows twice and is currently part of two anthologies, David Reuters' Outer Space/Inner Minds and Antologie Romana Australiana, a crosscultural work of dialogue and discourse between his Sydney workshop and the 'Palatul Culturii Bistrita-Romania' where he was translated into Romanian.

www.ingramcontent.com/pod-product-compliance
Lightning Source LLC
Chambersburg PA
CBHW051013050726
47592CB00007B/2825